Bounce Catch Kick Throw

Written by Janice Marriott
Illustrated by Peter Lubach

Contents

What is it?   2
All sorts of balls   5
Ball games   6
How to juggle   8
Bouncing balls   10
Make a bouncing ball   12
What makes a ball bounce?   14
Which ball bounces the highest?   16
Football   18
How a football is made   20
A quiz!   22
Index   23

Collins

What is it?

In this stadium, thousands of people are watching just one small thing.
What is it?

In the park, children are playing with one small thing.
What is it?

They are all watching or playing with a ball!

All sorts of balls

Some balls are good for bouncing...

... some for kicking ...

... or catching ...

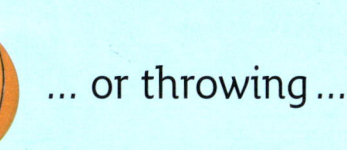

... or throwing ...

... or even for running with.

Ball games

Tennis

In most ball games, two or more people play with one ball.

Basketball

In juggling, one person plays with lots of balls!

Do you know how to juggle? It looks hard, but it's quite easy once you get used to it.

How to juggle

What you need:

- two balls

What you do:

Start with one ball.

1 Hold it in your right hand.

2 Throw it into your left hand.

3 Throw the ball back to your right hand.

4 Do this a few times, until you can catch the ball without dropping it!

Now try with two balls.

5 Hold one ball in each hand.

6 Throw ball 1, in your right hand, to your left hand.

7 When ball 1 is halfway between your right and left hands, throw ball 2 from your left hand to your right hand.

8 Catch ball 1 in your left hand.

9 Then catch ball 2 in your right hand.

10 Try to do this a few times without stopping.

Hey, now you're juggling!

Bouncing balls

Most balls can bounce ...

... but some are too heavy.

Cannon balls are heavy.

Some are too soft,
like a ball of wool ...

... or an old,
chewed tennis ball.

Make a bouncing ball

What you need:
- lots of wide rubber bands

What you do:
1. Get six rubber bands.
2. Fold them in half.

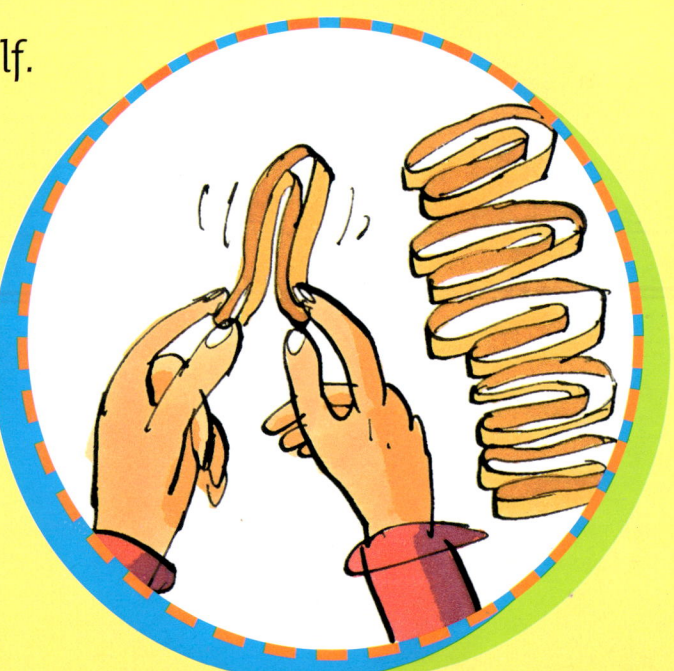

③ Put another rubber band around them.

④ Twist it around the six bands again until it is tight.

⑤ Now you have a lump of rubber bands that will become the middle of your ball.

⑥ Keep adding rubber bands, one at a time, until the ball is as big as you want.

Warning! This ball will be solid rubber. It will be quite heavy and **very** bouncy. Take it outside to play with. **Be careful!**

What makes a ball bounce?

Some balls are hard like your rubber band ball. A rubber band ball stretches and springs back into shape after it hits something solid, such as:

the ground ...

... a bat ...

... or a wall.

14

Some balls are full of air, like a football or tennis ball.

Air gets squashed inside a ball when it hits something.

When the air springs back it makes the ball bounce.

Which ball bounces the highest?

What you need:
- three balls – you can choose any balls you like
- three people
- a pencil
- a chart like this

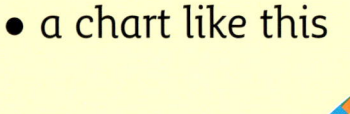

What you do:

1. One person stands up and drops one of the balls.

2. The second person checks where the ball bounces to. Does it bounce as high as the first person's knee, waist or head?

3. The third person marks the result on the chart.

4. Do the same with each ball.

Which ball bounced the highest?

17

Football

Football, or soccer, is the most popular ball game in the world.
It is played in nearly every country.

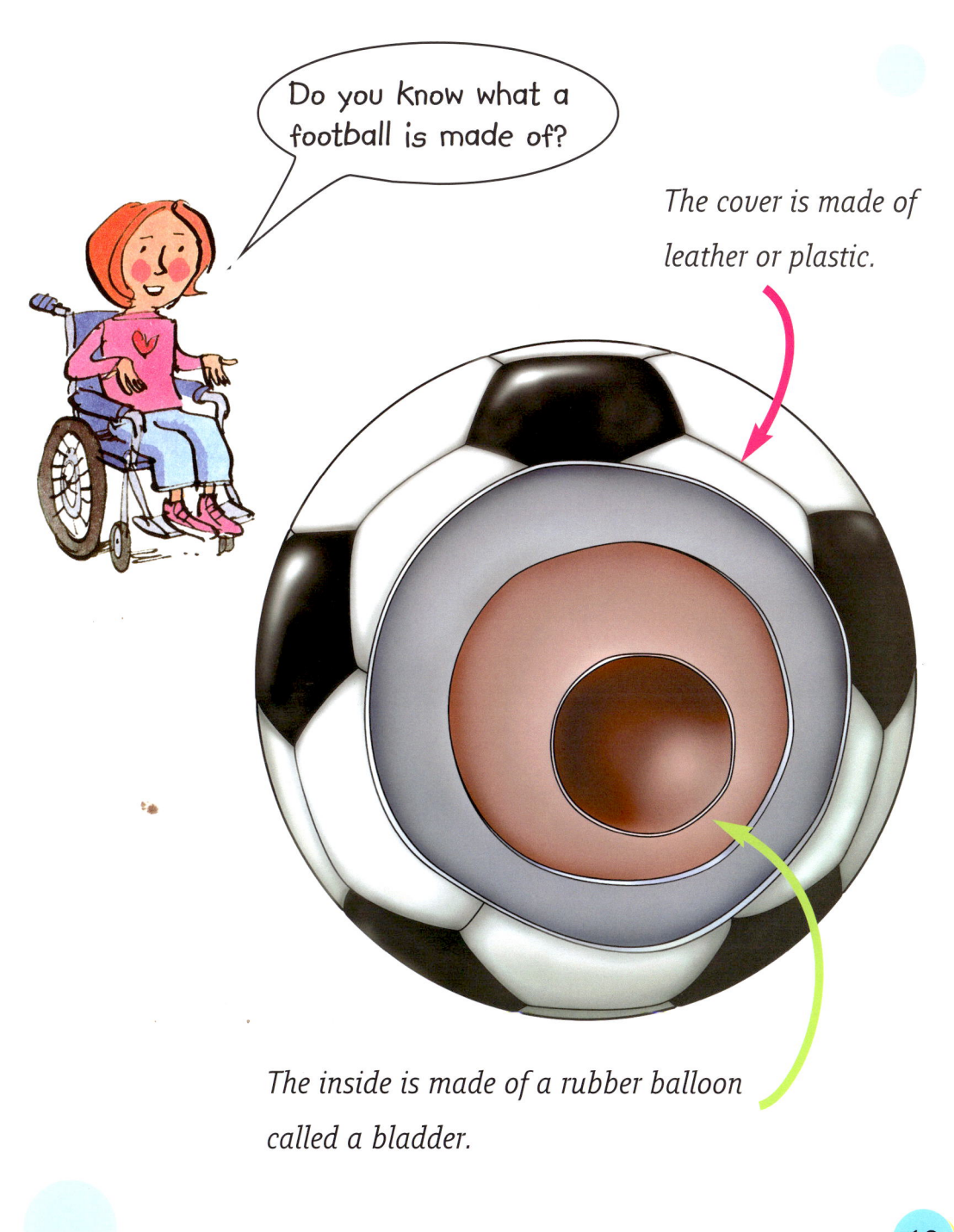

Do you know what a football is made of?

The cover is made of leather or plastic.

The inside is made of a rubber balloon called a bladder.

How a football is made

1 The cover material is cut into shapes.
Most balls use 32 shapes. Twenty of the shapes are six-sided. Twelve of the shapes are five-sided.

2 The shapes are sewn together.

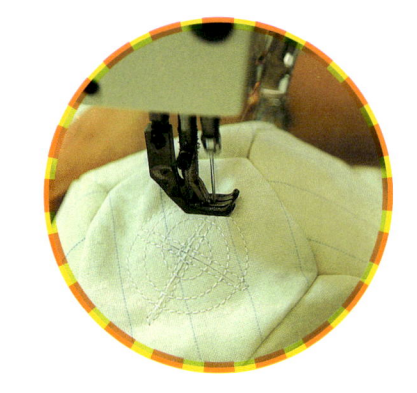

3 A rubber bladder is put inside the ball. Then the bladder is filled with air.

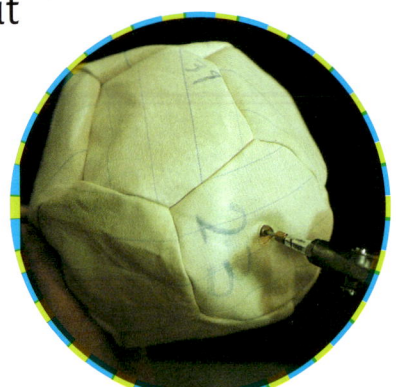

4 Now the football is ready to play with!

A quiz!

The answers are in the book!

1. What can you use to make a rubber ball?

2. Why do balls full of air bounce?

3. Which ball is too heavy to throw or kick?

4. Which balls don't bounce?

5. What is inside a football?

6. Which is the most popular ball game in the world?

7. Which game can one person play with lots of balls?

Index

air   15, 20

bouncing   10, 11, 12, 13, 14, 15

football   18, 19, 20, 21

games   6, 7, 18

juggling   7, 8, 9

making balls   12, 13, 20, 21

measuring bounce   16, 17

rubber bands   12, 13

soccer   18, 19, 20, 21

1 Elastic bands **2** Because the air inside them moves when they hit a solid surface. **3** A cannon ball **4** A cannon ball, a ball of wool, an old, chewed tennis ball **5** A rubber bladder **6** Football **7** Juggling

Ideas for guided reading

Learning objectives: Reading instructions for making something; noting the features of instructions; using the word ending 'ing' to support reading and spelling; listening to and following instructions.

Curriculum links: P.E: Games activities; Science: Forces and movement

Interest words: bounce, catch, kick, throw, playing, running, juggling, bladder, rubber, football

Resources: small whiteboards and pens

Word count: 643

Getting started

This book can be read over two sessions.

- Read the title together and discuss what type of text it is. It is a non-fiction book which contains instructions, general information and explanations.
- Ask children to find a page of instructions (pp 8-9, 12-13, 16-17). *What made them think they were instructions?*
- Ask them to find 'ing' words on p4 (*watching, playing*). These words are action words or verbs. What happens if we take away the *ing*? (The word still makes sense.)

Reading and responding

- Read pp2-4 together and discuss the pictures. *What do they remind you of?* (e.g. *Where's Wally?* or *Spot the Ball* in newspapers.)
- Then ask the children to read independently up to p21. Prompt the children to use a variety of cues to read unfamiliar words.
- Turn back to pp12-13 and look in more detail at the features of instructions, and discuss them (e.g. sets of instructions have a goal; they give a list of things you need; each instruction has a verb that tells you what to do and in what order, e.g. *get, fold, twist.*)